Eddie Askew

and daughters
Jenny Hawke with Stephanie Bell

··■■■··

Walking into the Light

A journey through grief in poems, prayers and thoughts

Other books by Eddie Askew
A Silence and a Shouting
Disguises of Love
Many Voices One Voice
No Strange Land
Facing the Storm
Breaking the Rules
Cross Purposes
Slower than Butterflies
Music on the Wind
Edge of Daylight (Memoirs)
Talking with Hedgehogs
Unexpected Journeys
Love is a Wild Bird
Encounters
Chasing the Leaves
Breaking Through
Dabbling with Ducks

Published, edited and distributed by TLM Trading Limited
0845 166 2253
www.tlmtrading.com

First Published 2009
Text by Eddie Askew and Jenny Hawke with Stephanie Bell
Paintings © A.D. (Eddie) Askew OBE

Design and production by Creative Plus Publishing Ltd,
www.creative-plus.co.uk

Printed and bound in India by Imago

ISBN 978-0-902731-76-9

Cover picture: Going Home, *watercolour*

Bible verses from the NIV (New International Version) used by permission of the
International Bible Society. Bible verse from The Message by Eugene Petersen,
published by Nav Press, used with permission. Bible verse from the
CEV (Contemporary English Version) used by permission of The Bible Society.

Dedication

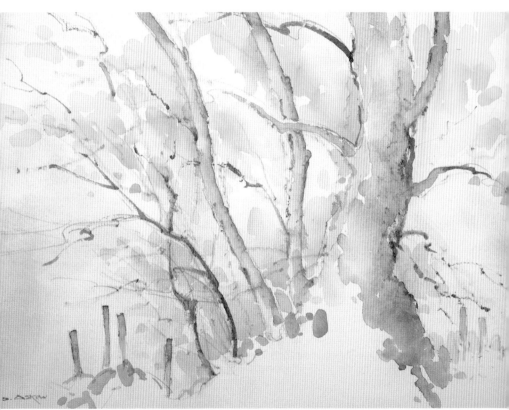

Autumn Light, *watercolour*

For our wonderful parents, with love and gratitude.

Introduction

Our father, Eddie Askew, died on the 27th September 2007 after a series of three strokes over a seven-week period. During that time, we had the privilege of being with him, caring for him, and being able to tell him what he meant to us as we prepared to say goodbye. None of that was easy, and at times it felt like our hearts were physically breaking, but looking back we realise we were in some way blessed.

Mum died seven months before Dad and, in a strange way, we found her death easier to process. She had struggled with the disability resulting from a serious stroke for over two years, and had had enough. She was ready to go, and the knowledge of that made it almost a release for both her and us.

· ■ ■ ■ ■ ■ ·

As we began the long process of dismantling a life's belongings, we came across these poems, which Dad had written for Mum after her death and just seven months before his own. They are beautiful, poignant and filled with such honesty and raw emotion, that they took our breath away. At first we wondered whether they were too private, too personal to be published, but then we found a scribbled note where Dad had written *'I hope that one day my experiences will help someone else'*, and this gave us his nod of approval to go ahead and publish the poems.

Dad faced grief head on and, as always, made something lasting and beautiful out of a tragic experience. As he grieved, we were aware of a subtle but tangible change in his paintings. Since Mum had her stroke, we all grieved for what she had lost and he began painting two people walking away into the distance, through gates, past a broken fence... it made me wonder. We began to recognise the reality of where they were in their lives. Dad talked about *painting your life story* and whether consciously or not, he was painting the change in theirs.

4

After her death, the paintings became more empty, the colours increasingly muted, with a stillness, a pause which quietly asked for your attention. Jenny asked Dad not to sell these paintings, to keep them for a book he might write about grief. He just smiled and said nothing, but after his death, she found them all kept carefully in a corner of the studio.

· ▪ ▮ ▰ ▮ ▪ ·

So, here they are, poems and paintings, extracts from his journal, thoughts and prayers from earlier books, put together in a way which we hope will help you as you follow your own path through grief. It is a long road, a painful journey but with moments of stillness, of beauty, and the possibility of a connection with something infinitely bigger than ourselves.

Jenny Hawke and Stephanie Bell, Summer 2009

Part One

We asked a stranger to take the photo. All ten of us, the whole family crammed together on a single slatted bench on the quay in Padstow, Cornwall; each of us laughing in the sun. It was 2003, May half-term week, and as usual, we were spending it together in a rented house on the edge of town.

Our days were filled with gentle walks, too much coffee and cake, and reading on the beach. Dad would sit and sketch. He hated walking and the beach! And in the evening, family meals with bottles of wine to smooth over heated philosophical debate, whilst the dogs sat under the table hoping for scraps.

We believed at some level that these times would last forever – year on year, building in enjoyment as the children grew and meshed together.

With the suddenness of a gust of cold wind, it changed. With one phone call from Dad, Mum's stroke became a reality in our lives.

· ▪ ■ ▓ ■ ▪ ·

Four years pass, December 2007, and we are on a flight to India, returning both Mum and Dads' ashes to the country they loved. A strange Christmas.

Every family has its story, and ours began in India, with Mum and Dad working for The Leprosy Mission in Purulia. Within a month of their wedding, they were on a ship heading for Bombay, beginning life as missionaries, Dad as a school teacher, and Mum always a strong presence helping and supporting him. We loved living there. It was our home, full of sun and unconditional love. We remember birthday parties in the large garden, feasts with the patients where we would eat wonderful curries on banana leaf plates, and sports days on the large field by the hospital. As we grew older, Steph and I went to boarding school in Darjeeling in the Himalayas, with Mum and Dad visiting for weeks at a time – a wonderful multi-racial school run by Christians. We were happy. By that time, Dad was the superintendent of the Leprosy Home and Hospital.

In 1965, we came back to England. Dad became the International Director of the Mission's worldwide operations and Mum began working for Baptist Church House in Holborn.

· ▪ ■ ▓ ■ ▪ ·

Years passed, the family grew as we married and had children, with Mum and Dad always there, always at the centre, our lives gently orbiting around theirs. We moved away to Surrey, they returned to Nottingham, the place of their childhood. They found a lovely bungalow on the edge of Attenborough Nature Reserve, a collection of former gravel pits, now a place of quiet waters, trees and wildlife.

Their days filled with involvement in their church, seeing friends, running retreats, painting, and walking the dog. We often had to book ahead to see them, their diaries so happily full. Recognition came with Dad's best selling books, his broadcasting and the OBE for services to leprosy. Theirs was a great love story, spanning over sixty years from the day they first met as teenagers at the local Baptist Church. Dad always said he only went there to meet the girls!

Time is precious, moment by moment, and now the eight of us, my sister Stephanie and I, our husbands Howard and Peter, our children, Claudia and Georgia, Jessamy and Samuel, continue to build on our memories. We are deeply aware of the heritage we have. We are so proud of our parents' lives, freely given in service to so many, thankful for the love Mum and Dad invested in us, and grateful for the legacy of creativity they left behind.

· ▪ ■ ▓ ■ ▪ ·

This book was conceived because of Dad's love of the written word. He had a special ability to condense his thoughts into simple but beautiful phrases, which so many of us can relate to. As we have grieved for them both over the last year, we have taken some comfort in reading through Dad's journal as he dealt with Mum's stroke, and then later, her death. Through it all neither Mum nor Dad lost their faith. They never turned away. Like the wild geese in Dad's book, *Facing the Storm*, they faced into the wind, waiting it out. They may have questioned, doubted, felt anger and despair in turn, but they never gave up. They recognised how hard life can be, and in faith, hoped for a way through.

Grieving is hard. It is a lonely road and when faced with a doubly significant loss, it feels the more shocking. A friend described it as 'seeing a different landscape'.

The world seems the same and yet everything has altered. The family dynamic has changed, and our foundations are shifting.

For us, our point of reference, our magnetic north, has gone and we are lost. And, for the moment, we remain so.

Extracts from Dad's journal

JOURNAL, 13TH JULY, 2004

THE STROKE

There's an adrenalin rush that keeps you going during the first
few hours.
The devastation.

Waking early, sensing that Barbara is awake beside me.
"Want a cuppa?" I ask.
The only reply, a moan. I reach over. Heavy, inert.
I get up quickly, walk around to the other side of the bed.
I realise the moan was an attempt to speak.
She struggles to move. Can't. Tries again, moans.

I know.
It's a stroke.

When Dad rang us to tell us the news, his concerns for us, as always, overrode what he knew was the seriousness of the stroke, wanting to reassure, to comfort us, even though he was the one in greater need.

Someone once said,
"Easy stuff is easy. How we deal with the tough stuff is what defines us.
How we stand and face it demonstrates, without words, who we really are."

· ▪ ■ ▉ ■ ▪ ·

Dad remained calm for us, in spite of the turmoil inside, sitting by her side, holding her hand, and just waiting. It was an activity we would have plenty of practice at over the coming months.

JOURNAL, ELEVEN PM
AFTER THE STROKE

Tears.
Bleak loneliness.
Late at night.

When she is in bed.
One millisecond
stole the life
we took for granted.
Love translated into emptiness.

Let anger loose
in a quiet room.

Anger at God –
if he is God he's big enough to take it –
and at the circumstances beyond control
turning life upside down,
dictating the future.

I hope and pray.
What else is there to do?

A.D.A.

Luke 10:33
But a Samaritan, as he travelled, came where the man was; and when he saw him, he took pity on him.

Life's gone a bit pear-shaped recently. My wife, Barbara, has been taken ill and had several weeks in Queen's Medical Centre in Nottingham. It started with an early morning 999 call. The ambulance rolled up – and soon she was blanketed, strapped in safely and on her way to hospital.

The paramedics were superb. Both men, really competent and very gentle. Reassuring too, all the way to Accident and Emergency. Then the organisation took over. Decisions all in other people's hands; people we didn't know, had never met before. We were no longer in charge of our own lives. We were fed into the system.

What impressed me most though, amid all the cool professionalism, was one paramedic. He was one of the two in the ambulance who'd answered our emergency call and delivered us to hospital. About an hour later, we were into all the tests and admission procedure when he walked back in, just to see how my wife was getting on. That was great. It wasn't part of his job to care like that, but he was concerned for her and perhaps a little for me.

In the tension and anxiety of the morning, I didn't remember his name. It was just one of those quiet acts of kindness that helped the day along. I hope someone shows him this page. I'd like to say thank you.

Lord, I thank you for the kindness of strangers. May I recognise your presence in their lives.

From Chasing the Leaves, *2005*

Dad often expressed his feelings in poetry and prayers. He also wrote some wonderful 'thoughts for the day' which were broadcast on Radio Nottingham and which later appeared in his books.

When Mum had her stroke, we grieved.
We grieved for the loss of part of our mother.
We grieved for the subtle change in her personality.
We wept for her inability to move, the unwelcome weakness in her body that
came quietly in the night.

We saw the confusion in her eyes, and the stoic refusal to complain.
Slowly we seemed to adjust, although every visit brought a fresh reminder of the
impact on their lives.

Time passed.
Dad was silently angry with the momentous change that came with the bursting of
one small blood vessel.

And we prayed.
As he said, what else was there to do?

**Lord, there is no one else that we can go to!
Your words give eternal life. We have faith in you, and we are
sure that you are God's Holy One.
John 6:68-69 (CEV)**

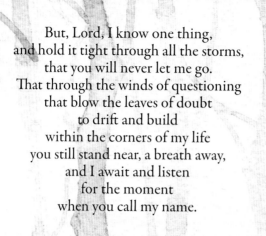

But, Lord, I know one thing,
and hold it tight through all the storms,
that you will never let me go.
That through the winds of questioning
that blow the leaves of doubt
to drift and build
within the corners of my life
you still stand near, a breath away,
and I await and listen
for the moment
when you call my name.

From Encounters, *2004*

A. D. ASKEW

A Rainy Day, *watercolour*

Matthew 11:28
"Come to me, all you who are weary and burdened, and I will give you rest."

Driving along the other day, I saw something on the road. Just a tatty plastic shopping bag. Too many of them around, I thought. As I drove over it – no, I couldn't stop to tidy it up, there were other cars behind me – the wind whipped it up into the air. The last I saw of it, in the rear-view mirror, it was dancing in the slipstream of my car. It swirled high, then down and sideways like a manic seagull, until the following car caught it and started the process all over again. The bag was off once more, whipped along by forces it couldn't control.

I've been feeling a bit like that since Barbara, my wife, has been in hospital. Events have been happening beyond my control. I've had to rely on other people, doctors, nurses, physiotherapists, and never been quite sure what would happen next. Far from sorting things out myself, the way I like to do, other people have been in control both of Barbara's life and mine.

Blown around like that plastic bag I seemed helpless and not a lot of use, but the feeling doesn't last. First, I thank God there are others to take control when I'm out of my depth – the professionals. Then, there are the friends who step in and lighten the burden, and say those words that mean so much, "We're thinking of you, and praying for you." That's great.

Lord of uncertainty, when I am pushed around and don't know where to turn, help me to trust you with my worries.

From Chasing the Leaves, *2005*

The extract opposite was in Dad's journal on the third day after Mum's stroke.

JOURNAL, 16TH JULY, 2004

Psalm 145:1-9
I will exalt you, my God the King;
I will praise your name for ever and ever.
Every day I will praise you
and extol your name for ever and ever.
Great is the LORD and most worthy of praise;
his greatness no one can fathom.
One generation will commend your works to another;
they will tell of your mighty acts.
They will speak of the glorious splendour of your majesty,
and I will meditate on your wonderful works.
They will tell of the power of your awesome works,
and I will proclaim your great deeds.
They will celebrate your abundant goodness
and joyfully sing of your righteousness.
The LORD is gracious and compassionate,
slow to anger and rich in love.
The LORD is good to all;
he has compassion on all he has made.

These are words and promises of great comfort but they also
challenge us. Compassion, in circumstances like these?
Lord, I don't blame You for her stroke. I've believed for years in the
randomness of suffering caused by an imperfect world, but I still
would like to see less randomness in the outcome....

JOURNAL, 19TH JULY, 2004

I've just cleaned the loo, washed the hand basins, hoovered the
dog hairs off the sitting room carpet. I usually hoover but not
the other things but while B is in hospital, it's me or chaos. I'll try
to keep chaos at bay.
While polishing the hand basins, I said quietly, "This is for you, love"
and it began to get personal. She'll probably never know - although
I'm quite likely to boast about it sometime in the future - but
suddenly there seemed to be real value in it. It's something B does
every day, for me, but as the circumstances are reversed I thought
of George Herbert's hymn.... "Make the drudgery divine."

JOURNAL, 20TH JULY, 11.30PM

When I go to bed, that's when the darkness tries to hit. Lonely, sad, not for myself, but thinking of B and how she's in this condition.

I sit on the edge of the bed and pray. Not with words, just surrounding her with my love, God's love, hoping, hoping... hoping...

JOURNAL, 22ND JULY, 2004

THE CREDIBILITY GAP – Between what you write and preach and affirm that you believe. – (the ease with which you pray and leave so-and-so in God's hands) and the hard reality of seeing someone you love deeply, lying helplessly, totally dependant.

When is an act of faith real, when is it a cop out?
Each day I look for the smallest bit of progress, grab it, and hold hard.

Lord, I need you now.
Not as a refuge.
Not as a dream.
As a companion.
As someone to walk with me on the road.

From A Silence and a Shouting, *1982*

Psalm 130:5
I wait for the LORD, my soul waits, and in his word I put my hope. My soul waits for the LORD' more than watchmen wait for the morning... (NIV)

Queen's Medical Centre, F floor. I was waiting for a lift to take me down to the main entrance on B. I'm past walking down the stairs for four floors even if the alternative is to wait. There are three lifts on every landing, but when I press the little button on the wall the lifts are usually well down at ground level. All you can do is stand and stare at the three closed doors, and wait. Then, like the proverbial buses, two lifts come together.

Sometimes, wherever we are, all we can do is wait. We may feel we need to move on from where we are, but doors seem to be firmly shut. However hard we wish to change things, we just have to wait. It's out of our hands. Waiting's often harder than doing, but we don't get anywhere banging on the wall or repeatedly ringing the bell. The lift will come when it's good and ready, and bring with it new opportunities.

Maybe the waiting time's been given to encourage us to think things through a bit more carefully.

And when the lift finally arrives we have a choice. Ignore it, or step into it, press a button, and hope it'll take us where we want to go.

Life's a bit like that.

Lord of time and eternity, stand with me when the waiting's hard, and teach me patience. But do it gently please.

From Chasing the Leaves, *2005*

A new way of life

People say that you can get used to anything, but is that really true? We are used to each other as we are, as we have always been, especially our parents. They are the strong ones, the ones we can count on, depend upon. When change comes, expectations remain embedded at a deep level, and only time and gentleness will ease us through the difficult transition.

We were the cared for; now we are the carers.

I, Jenny, remember visiting Mum on the ward, finding her halfway through a walk with her physiotherapist, Christine. She encouraged me to take Mum's hand and help her. I took her hand as I always have done, when Mum was leading me. Christine gently pointed out that I needed to change my handhold, alter my grip, so that I could lead her. I felt something pierce my heart as I realised our roles had changed forever. I did not want them to.

JOURNAL, 28TH JULY, 2004

You wake up one morning and find your world has collapsed. Nothing has its usual meaning. You're adrift in uncertainty. Things, people, conditions which you have assumed are given constants are no longer valid, no longer to be taken for granted. You live in the day – exist would be more accurate – not daring, not able, to look any further ahead.

JOURNAL, 6TH AUGUST, 2004

The strange thing is that when I am most angry at God, I still go back to Him to tell Him I'm angry. Somehow, He doesn't let go.

The carpet's been pulled out from underneath us, and we're left facedown in the wreckage of a spoiled lifestyle.

How to pick up the pieces – and reassemble them.

Maybe we would be wrong to try to reassemble them as they were; more that we have to use the pieces which are left and whatever new pieces we are given to build something different, and tolerable – even happy.

Lord, take my anger. Nail it to your cross.
And fill the space it leaves with your love.
It's a big space. It will take some filling.

From A Silence and a Shouting, *1982*

JOURNAL, 19TH AUGUST, 2004

In the quiet, late at night I simply sit to pray without words. Just "bathe B in love". Surround her in love in my thoughts and just hold her there.

In the quiet of that moment, I realised (or the Spirit prompted me? I don't know) that there's no point asking to understand why? There's no sensible human/God answer, other than the random working out of natural laws. Something I've held for years, but harder when it happens.

No point in trying to understand, just look for the strength to cope with the reality, and find an acceptance of the situation.

How easy to say; and what goes on in B's mind in trying to come to terms with it?

Then, Lord, without words, in the stillness
you are there ...
And I love you.
Lord, teach me to pray.

From A Silence and a Shouting, *1982*

Oxfordshire Farm

John 16:33
I have told you these things, so that in me you may have peace. In this world you will have trouble. But take heart! I have overcome the world. (NIV)

While Barbara was in hospital recently, she lost her wristwatch. It was only a cheap Timex. I'd bought it for her so that she could leave her good watch at home. Just as well, or she'd have lost the good one. I asked around, nursing staff, cleaners, no one had seen it. Not in the bathroom or under her pillow, nowhere. "Ah well," I thought, "It's no big deal." Illness tends to put things into a different perspective.

Back home, I started to unload the washing machine – amazing how domesticated I'm getting – all the clothes I'd brought home from the hospital. As I took out the last towel, I heard something rattle. I looked into the machine, felt around with my hand, and there was Barbara's watch. I'm not quite sure how it got there. I think she'd put it into a pocket and forgotten, and I hadn't gone through the pockets before putting the clothes in the washer.

Anyway, there it was. A bit of the strap was frayed, the plastic cover slightly scratched, but it still told the time. Totally immersed in hot water and soap, spun at 1400 revs per minute, it still worked. Something I needed to take to heart. Barbara's been going through the mill with her stroke but, hopefully, when we've worked through all the struggle and anxiety, she'll come out at the other end, maybe more careworn than she was, but still in working order. And that will be because of all the TLC – the tender, loving care – she's getting, even though at times it feels like going through the wringer. But then, Jesus knew all about that.

Lord of life, it's not easy, I confess, to live the peace you offer, but with your help I'll make it through another day.

From Chasing the Leaves, 2005

Lord, when I'm tempted to give up and turn away, just let me see you on the road ahead of me.

From Love is a Wild Bird, 2003

JOURNAL, 28TH AUGUST, 2004

I had Radio 4 on as a background, the usual Sunday service.
"O Love that wilt not let me go, I rest my weary soul in Thee ...."
A lovely old hymn, by Matheson; the words come seeping back, not in
complete sentences but enough to floor me.
"I give Thee back the life I owe" ... "that seekest me through rain..."
The tiredness and tension of the week suddenly hits and
I begin to weep.
I got an old hymn book and looked it up.
Such lovely optimistic words. Words of faith and a life surrendered...
I'm not there yet. All I can do is put a qualification before the
phrases: I try to rest my weary soul in Thee.
                I try to.....
That's the best I can offer. It should be enough.
The desire to desire....

*Lord, sometimes my burdens seem too heavy and my energy too light.
But if you'll take the other end I'll try to lift my share.*

From Chasing the Leaves, 2005

JOURNAL, 1ST SEPT, 2004

"...the back turned toward Ireland,
Farewell to the known and dear,
Advance to the unknown,
With it's formidable hazards,
Its sharp demands."
Columba

I was rather down this morning, apprehensive of the demands that
would be made on me today (And what about Barbara?).

Opened my book of Celtic Prayer hoping for some reassurance and
read these words of Columba. A challenge more than a comfort.
Maybe that's what I need, although it's not what I'd like or want.
It' a case of "one day at a time". How easy it is to say....

JOURNAL, 5TH SEPTEMBER, 2004

I've been asking myself the impossible question.
Why pain, illness, stroke etc? Why B and not me?
No answer of course. Theology hits reality with a thud. The only
thing that makes it acceptable is randomness. The theologies don't
wash - I find acceptance very difficult - yet I keep coming back to
the God I'm angry with in prayer.

Someone once said,
"If you want to make God smile, tell Him your plans."

Dad was never afraid to ask questions of his faith, and face his doubts. He always said he was deeply suspicious of people who felt they had their faith all sewn up, and were in possession of all the answers.

JOURNAL, 16TH NOVEMBER, 2004

As I write this, I find today I cannot believe in a loving God.
I've been hovering on the brink of this for some time, not daring
to face it.
Preparing B. for bed, she was racked with a sudden heart-rending
outburst of deep sobbing tears - no reason, pure misery. If belief is
to be restored, I need some reassurance. I am deeply disturbed.
What is it all about?

Within minutes, B is normal. "It's just the illness" - but why?
Getting her to bed, she asked for some cream on an aching shoulder.
As I massaged it in, something in me said, "Your hand is the evidence
of that loving God." But that kindness anyone would do! Yes, that
suggests no limits on God's presence and work. But... still... what good
are strokes? How fair is this sort of suffering?
Either God has to work harder on me or I have to work harder on
my faith! Though even a mustard seed of faith seems too great a
demand on me at the moment.

A new way of coping

Weeks changed to months as they tried to come to terms with what had happened. As Dad said, in one split second, everything had changed. Once Mum came home from hospital, Dad became her full-time carer. He struggled at first to carry on writing and painting, but he found a way. When Mum was resting, he would creep into the studio and paint. When awake, she seemed to need the reassurance of his presence so he bought a laptop, and sat at the kitchen table where she could see him, and he continued to write. He wrote two more books in the months that followed and preserved his sense that life could still in some way be "normal". We think it saved his sanity, in fact we are sure of it.

They tried to enjoy life in a different way, with the support of their church, friends and neighbours, always grateful for phone calls, visits, and many small acts of kindness. Life moved on through 2005 and 2006. Mum went to a local, friendly day centre twice a week. Dad continued to show his love and care for her through what were difficult times, worrying about whether he was caring for her properly. Suffering guilt when he found it hard to adjust to her needs and limitations.

JOURNAL, NEW YEAR'S DAY, 2007

We wish each other a Happy New Year. Is it possible? Who knows? Barbara continues up (mostly) and down. Before supper – tears, for "no reason". Going to bed, she makes jokes, including one about "only having the use of one arm", the first time I have heard her acknowledge the fact. A coming to terms with it?
I feel unstable. Mostly coping, but recently music of all sorts has made me very tearful, anything that I can associate with B, our relationship and love, and any hopes for the future. It all seems so bleak, and I feel very sad and disturbed for B. What quality of life does she have, can she have, will she have?
Happy New Year? (And what quality of life do I have?)

JOURNAL, 7TH JANUARY, 2007, 3.45PM.

As I came back into the sitting room from the kitchen, I went up to B as she sat on the sofa, bent over, put my hands on her shoulders and asked gently, "How are you doing?"
She looked me in the eyes and replied, "I wish I knew."
Regret, realism, two-and-a-half years of ups and downs, pain.
The forgetfulness doesn't seem to deal with the anxiety.
It was an occasional return to the real world

Part Two

After two years of this different life, Dad continued to do all he could. We visited and phoned often, painfully aware of Dad's growing tiredness and Mum's stoic and silent acceptance. It was hard to see them living with such limitations. It was especially hard to see how our spirited, warm and capable mother had shrunk to a small, and at times, bewildered old lady. We felt angry at the unfairness of it all. Both in their 80s, we had hoped for a kinder end to their working lives. But the idea of fairness often disappoints.

· ▪ ▪ ▪ ▪ ·

Mum collapsed at home on the 18th February, 2007. She was taken into the Queen's Medical Centre, Nottingham, and diagnosed as having had a serious heart attack. In the emergency room, she quietly told me, Jenny, that she had had enough. They had both made living wills to record their wish not to be resuscitated if they were really ill. We made sure the doctors knew that she did not want intervention and she was made comfortable.

The next day, the whole family arrived to see her. During that hour, it was as if the stroke had never happened; a brief window had opened and the old Mum was back. She was alert, she looked normal, laughed and joked with all of us and had something special to say to each one. We believe she knew she was going and was saying goodbye. We laughed and took photos, possibly bizarre in the circumstances, but we wanted to freeze the moment and be reminded of the great character we were saying goodbye to.

· ▪ ▪ ▪ ▪ ·

The next day I felt an urgency to visit her a second time, having already been in once. She was sleepy but in no pain. I sat by her side, holding her hand, and I began to quietly sing all her favourite hymns. *Blessed Assurance, Amazing Grace, The Lord's my Shepherd*. At times she joined in. I read the 23rd Psalm, and parts of the last chapters of Revelation to her.

After an hour or so, I told her I was leaving. I kissed her goodbye and she said, "Yes, off you go; full of the Spirit. We have had such a good time."

She died the next morning at 3.32 a.m. Dad and I were with her; Steph was awake in London, praying for her. Two other friends were also sleepless, and praying.

She was not alone.

Dad contacted many people with the news of Mum's death. His email announcement was short, stark, and made us weep.

At 3.30 a.m. Barbara passed away, quietly, with no pain and with great dignity.

And I thought I heard the sound of trumpets and Barbara saying, "That must be someone important." And it was.

> Lord, take my hand
> and hold me in the dark
> when I can't see the way ahead.
> And if at times I stumble,
> as I know I will,
> tighten your grip on me
> and don't let go.
>
> *From* Encounters, *2004*

The Annunciation, *watercolour*

JOURNAL, EASTER 2007

QUESTION

I do not argue with the
process –
birth, life, and death –
the orderly progression
to death's inevitability.
I simply question the pain.
The pain of loss.
A God of love you say
and yet the more one loves
the greater is the hurt
at parting.
Birth's pain is soon forgotten
in new life's joy
but there is little comfort
in the losing
and pious words, well meant,
just fall on stony ground
and wither.

Time heals, I'm told
but each day's dawn
repeats the grief.
The open wound
rubbed raw still bleeds.
And holding on to faith
asks almost more than
I can give.
Lord, I believe, but only just.
Yesterday's promises
taste stale.
All I can offer is what I am,
you'll have to be content
with that.

Eddie Askew

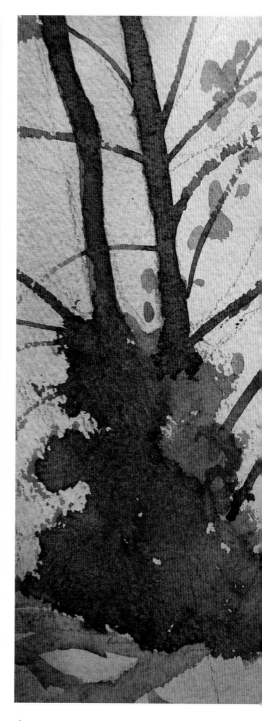

Sunset, *watercolour*

The Funeral

Planning a funeral is never easy. In the planning, we are forced to face the loss of the person, and the finality of death, whilst we are still in shock.

We found it helpful and somehow calming to look through the richness of Scripture, poetry and other sources to find words and music which reflected Mum's love of life, her vibrancy and the strength of her faith. Bible passages from Job, Daniel, Isaiah and Hebrews, and the final page of *Pilgrim's Progress* were all comforting and might be words that will help you too.

I know that my Redeemer lives, and that in the end he will stand upon the earth. And after my skin has been destroyed, yet in my flesh I will see God; I myself will see him with my own eyes – I, and not another. How my heart yearns within me!
Job 19: 25-27 (NIV)

Men and women who have lived wisely and well will shine brilliantly, like the cloudless, star-strewn night skies. And those who put others on the right path to life will glow like stars forever.
Daniel 12:3 (The Message)

Do you not know? Have you not heard? The LORD is the everlasting God, the Creator of the ends of the earth. He will not grow tired or weary, and his understanding no-one can fathom. He gives strength to the weary and increases the power of the weak. Even youths grow tired and weary, and young men stumble and fall; but those who hope in the LORD will renew their strength. They will soar on wings like eagles; they will run and not grow weary, they will walk and not be faint.
Isaiah 40:28-31 (NIV)

Then your light will break forth like the dawn, and your healing will quickly appear; then your righteousness will go before you, and the glory of the LORD will be your rear guard. Then you will call, and the LORD will answer; you will cry for help, and he will say: Here am I.
Isaiah 58:8-9 (NIV)

I see myself now at the end of my Journey, my toilsome days are ended. I am going now to see that Head that was crowned with Thorns, and that Face that was spit upon for me. I have formerly lived by Hear-say and Faith, but now I go where I shall live by sight, and shall be with him in whose Company I delight myself. I have loved to hear my Lord spoken of; and wherever I have seen the print of His shoe in the earth, there have I coveted to set my foot too.
From Pilgrim's Progress by John Bunyan

We also sang her favourite hymns, taking comfort in the familiarity of the words, often sung before in India in a small dark chapel in the Leprosy Hospital grounds in Purulia.

It was bittersweet, knowing that she was no longer restricted by the stroke, but awed by the depth of love Dad had for her, and the pain he was feeling.

The celebration of her life followed, with photos of happier times throughout her life. Each person in the family contributed, the youngest, Georgia and Claudia, reading poems they had written. Dad spoke of her as "the love of his life", remembering sixty years before, their walk to the bus stop, and their first kiss. He said, "We missed the next three buses."

We remembered how we would often ring her but because she was so eager to talk, we would forget what we wanted to say. She always said her epitaph would be: 'Here lies Barbara. She talked a lot.'

We gave time for friends to speak with an 'open mike' and people gave their recollections, full of laughter through years of knowing her. And we had a book of remembrance by the door for anyone to write in a memory or thought for us to read later.

JOURNAL, 1ST MARCH, 2007

I feel deeply sad. Today was Barbara's funeral. I can hardly write that without crying. It is so final in the earthly sense, and I can only cling to the faith that it isn't the end of our love. That in some real sense I shall know/sense/feel her loving presence after death. And she me. The funeral was inspiring, affecting as it would be. The words Steph put together – very sensitive and helpful. But I could hardly look at the coffin without crying.

When it was all over the family returned home to us in Attenborough (that should be me – I have to learn) – noisy talk, noisy TV, noise, noise.
All I wanted was quiet.
Quiet to think over the day, to lick my wounds. Anything but noise! But their presence meant love and support.
Now 23:15 p.m. I'm exhausted.

JOURNAL, 5TH MARCH, 2007

THE AFTERLIFE

I picture a state of being where good is constantly happening, where God remains invisible (we humans anthropomorphise him, but God is not human) but constantly at work in me, loving even the worst to become the best.
But that leaves as many questions as answers. Have started reading the Psalms again – such a mixture of worship, anger, feelings of abandonment, whistling in the dark. "God will come to my rescue and punish the evil" – yes, so it says.

LETTING GO

Yet another card with sympathy. Folk talk about "the need to let go" of the loved one. I don't want to let go. Let go the body, the shell, yes, but not the memories – not the picture of her face, so still – that's a precious picture I want to keep.

"To see God's face" Psalm 17 can't be taken literally – God doesn't have a face or a body.

On days when I sat with B after her stroke I hoped and prayed that she would die first – thinking I'd be best able to cope with the grief and loneliness. I wonder now.

V. early days, but how long will this intense grief last? Do I have to let go before I sail into quieter waters? How long?

I can't settle.

I can't settle to anything. I begin a job – tidying some papers; give up, sit and stare into space. I thought I might go to church but I can't raise the energy.

There seems little space left for God. I'm sure some folks (like B) have an unshakeable faith whatever comes. I don't. I'm willing to believe it's _me_ at fault, not allowing him/her/it to get a foothold (how can feet hold?) or any space or time.

I'll try the Psalms again.

I STILL PRAY.

I still pray but it's an exercise of the will – no joy in it, no conversation, just a monologue by me. Where is God when it hurts? The normal answer is 'within the pain', sharing it with the sufferer – me. (That may satisfy theologically, but it doesn't help. I seem to want a good fairy, not a grown-up God.) But at least I am still talking to him/her/it, even though there is no answer.

JOURNAL, 9TH MARCH, 2007

THE ASHES

I don't know what to write.
I've been to the undertakers to pay
their bill and collected Barbara's ashes.
All very hushed and reverent - in a
dark green substantial cardboard box.
Bigger and heavier than I thought.
I was surprised by the weight.
As I unlocked our front door, things
become emotional.

I welcomed her home - but it's not her.
She is ...? With God, or asleep, or ...?
These ashes represent 63 years of
loving life and now I've got them - got
all that remains physically of B - I
don't know what to do with them.
I've prayed for B over them, I've told
her I love her, and now, gently, I've
put her/them in a cupboard in our
bedroom.

And I've realised that the cliché is
true - love is stronger than death.

I still love her, I know I always will,
death cannot cancel it, change it.

Hallelujah.

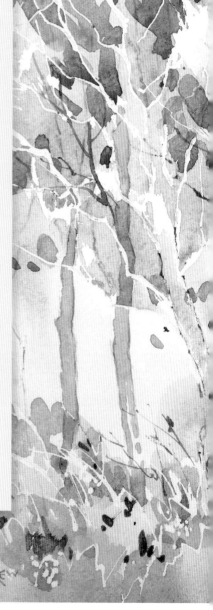

A.D. ASKEW

32

Tanglewood, *watercolour*

The distressing decision to empty her wardrobes

We did it together, reliving memories as we saw the colours and patterns taking us back to sunnier days. We laughed as we discovered so many clothes, in so many places.

The letting go of possessions, the loosening of ties has to be done, but now I wonder if we were a little hasty, perhaps we needed more time to look, to touch and process more gently.

There is no rush on this painful path and regret can be a harsh companion. We must learn to be kind to ourselves. This might be a decision you need to make in the future. Go gently and do things in a way that feels right to you, with no rush, leaving no place which regret might later fill.

Taking Flight, *watercolour*

On the Third Day

The empty wardrobe
its web of coat hangers dangling uselessly
mirrors the emptiness inside.
The shelf paper curling at the edges
scuffed where shoes have stood
waiting for her to choose the pair
she would wear today.
But they have gone.
The shoes, together with the clothes,
to an Oxfam welcome.

Tears come uninvited
but welcome in the knowledge they will bring release.

A short relief,
a temporary catharsis on the path.
A road lonely, companionate no more.

I too am emptied, my purposes black-bagged and binned.
I pray.
I struggle to thank God for answered prayers.
Believing it was for the best, her best.
We let her go, and seeing her so still and free from pain,
gently she went,
one moment here,
the next no sign except the stillness of her last goodbye.

I wept.

I weep still.

And wait in hope the day may come
when I may laugh again,
when memories of shared love
may fill the emptiness of my life
if not to overflowing
at least to make the emptiness more bearable.
Until one day of resurrection.

Eddie Askew

Early days

During these early days, Dad bravely faced a knee replacement operation, only two weeks after the funeral. It had been booked for many months. Dad told me later, "I put my grieving on hold when I was in the hospital. I couldn't think of it. I needed to get through the op."

We sometimes have to let life get in the way, and pause in our grieving process. Then when we can, we pick it up again, and continue. Even the doctor warned when prescribing temporary sleeping medication, "It will stop you grieving, you know..."

The important thing is just to continue.

· ▪ ▊ ▊ ▪ · ·

Dad kept his wonderful sense of humour, and recorded thoughts that had made him laugh, all his books are full of them.
Here's one that must have struck a chord with him at about the time his knees were giving him trouble –

A centipede developed arthritis. In great pain that involved his many joints, he sought out the Master – the expert with solutions to all problems – and asked his advice. The Master thought for a while and then offered the suggestion, that the centipede became a squirrel.
The centipede was delighted with the idea, and said,
 "Great! How do I become a squirrel?"
 "Oh" said the Master, "I only provide the solutions, implementation is your problem."

JOURNAL, 21ST APRIL, 2007

LONELINESS

I used to love having a day or two or three, on my own. It was a chance to think, to be, to read, to write, paint - whatever.

Now I am on my own - and it stretches out in front of me. Time to paint, to write but the energy is not there. No one, i.e. B, to bounce ideas off, to show my latest painting, to ask her to read something I'd written.

Life tends to be grey, monochromatic, the colours gone out of it. (I suppose part of it is in the fact that I can't move far, I'm careful not to damage my new knee.)
Even God is monochrome. How to get the colour back?

JOURNAL, 22ND APRIL, 2007

Last night I picked up one of my books, 'Facing the Storm'. I opened it at random and found a piece titled 'Resting in God'.
One phrase grabbed my attention.
'But in the end, the relationship between God and me has to go beyond that - to resting. Learning simply to sit with him, quietly. Leaving the final decisions with Him.'

I've not got there yet. I'm hanging on to Barbara, my mental image, my memories. It's almost as though letting go is abandoning her, even though it's letting go to God. And I suspect letting go is the mechanism by which we take up the threads of ordinary life and re-balance.

Resting in God

Be still, and know that I am God. Psalm 46:10 (NIV)

A church minister was being interviewed on television. His wife had been a deacon in the Anglican Church. She had died, just two weeks earlier. The day she was ordained she had been told she had leukaemia.

"After the initial shock," he said, "she made it clear she didn't agree with God about it."

I warmed to that. Our discipleship shouldn't make us unthinking zombies, accepting everything that happens without question. We have a right, even a duty, to use the minds God gave us. Not simply repeat the well-worn platitudes.

"Did prayer help?" he was asked. A thoughtful pause. "Yes ...but don't ask me how. Prayer is learning to rest in God."

Resting in God. After the questioning, and not necessarily getting the answer you want, or think you need, resting in him is all there is. Leaving it with him even when we disagree. Relying on his love.

I get less and less satisfied with the sort of prayer that's constant petition. Of course asking is part of prayer, but it tends to take over. I suspect it's the activist in us – we want things done, decisions made, goals accomplished.

But in the end, the relationship between God and me has to go beyond that – to resting. Learning simply to sit with him, quietly. Leaving the final decisions to him. They're his anyway, and if he's not competent to deal with them, nobody is.

From Facing the Storm, *1989*

Lord, if it's questions you want I've got them.
Bucketsful.
I'm like someone just out of depth,
standing on tiptoe,
the tide sucking away the sand from under my feet.
My arms stretched out,
just above the waterline of doubt.
The water's cold, it slaps my face.
Another wave and I'll go under.

But when I pause, take breath so shakily,
I think, perhaps if I asked less
there'd be more time to hear your answers.
My mind's so full of self-created doubts
there's little space for you.

Part of the trouble, Lord,
is that I want life tidy.
Secure. Predictable. And that's not how you work.
I've found that out, painfully at times.
I've got the scars to prove it.
But occasionally I find the honesty
to say that you're in charge.

And so I ask, Lord,
not necessarily to understand
the way things are,
but just to find the grace to rest in you.
To let my problems wait.
To still my mind
and in the blessed peace and quiet
that comes when I relax,
and lift my arms,
surrender to your presence.
And in your nearness
find that's all I need.

From Facing the Storm, *1989*

Flower Market, *watercolour*

40

Saturday's Flowers

I bought flowers
every Saturday morning
from the stall in the square.
They were the colour of love.
You always smiled and thanked me
"They're nice," you said.
Flowers fade.
Petals drop uncounted.
She loves me,
she loves me not,
always the last petal counted the love
although I did not need
the flower's reassurance.

I shall continue
to buy flowers
every Saturday morning
at the stall in the square.
And I shall listen
for her voice
saying "Thank you."

Eddie Askew, 2007

Emptiness

One of the things which often distressed Dad in those early months was the habitual turning to her chair, only to be met with emptiness. The desire to share, to tell a joke, to finish the crossword, habits developed over years of loving and living.

We would speak at the end of each day and I would hear his sadness. His excitement at seeing two small ducks arriving at the pond in their garden turned to pain as he ran in to get his camera. He wanted to take a photo so that he could show Mum.

And again, he remembered.
This slow unravelling of a lifetime of habits.

· ■ ■ ▓ ■ ■ ·

The Chair

I turn to speak to her.

She is not there.

The chair is empty.

Eddie Askew, 2007

· ■ ■ ▓ ■ ■ ·

We experience the same now, having lost them both. So often, as if our unconscious mind does not yet know they are gone, we move to the phone. To share some news, to ask advice. But then the realisation floods in, unwelcome but persistent.

They are gone.

We wonder when it will begin to feel like reality.

Silence

Silence echoes round the room,
tangible, terrible.
No comfort in it as there once was.
It had been a silence of mutuality
when looks spoke
and laughed and loved.
No need for words.
Now the silence is the other.
It cries out noiselessly
for words to comfort,
to reassure
that all is well with her.
To warm the silent ice
that chills the spirit.
O for just one word.

Eddie Askew, 2007

43

Friday 11th May, 2007

Dad met up with friends – a discussion ensues on church, life and Christianity. One friend said that in listening to Jesus, she "was waiting for the Lord to tell her what he wanted her to do next."

Dad suggested she tell the Lord what she wanted to do, and see how he reacts. She seemed quite surprised.

JOURNAL, 13TH MAY, 2007

WHY DOES GOD MAKE LOVING SO PAINFUL?

When I took Kathryn, our minister, to lunch I asked her that question, she suggested that the greater the pain the greater one's capacity to feel joy. I didn't go along with that!

But thinking it through I turned it round and asked myself would I be willing to lose the joys if that meant there'd be less or no pain? The answer is a clear No – I'll accept the pain – although I still don't understand, and thank God for the joys. Light and dark.

JOURNAL, 30TH MAY, 2007

BLESSED BEYOND MEASURE

The family are wonderful – their loving care touches me deeply. I am blessed 'beyond measure.'

And yet I carry a heaviness around, a weight of loss. I'm gradually getting more positive but it's a struggle. I am grateful but I'm without B. There's a strong truth in 'God gives, God takes away' although he doesn't do it deliberately – it's just part of life – the cycle of living and dying. I thank God for all the years we were together. Such love and blessing beyond value ... Deo Gratias.

Last thought – I reckon the above is maybe the best prayer I've said for a long time.

JOURNAL, 3RD JUNE, 2007

SHE'LL BE BACK SOON

Later the day changed. I kept feeling B was present and I was talking to her. Then a slight change. "She'll be back soon," I kept thinking. (It hurt and depressed me. I thought I was more in equilibrium than that.)

JOURNAL, 7TH JUNE, 2007

JULIAN FELLOWSHIP MEETING.

This morning, here at home. I led. I sat quietly, as always, just being. But thoughts came unbidden.

My faith's taken a hammering over B's death – anger, rebelliousness over the stroke etc., questions without answers ... recently in prayer, I've asked for faith to be strengthened.

This morning, in quiet, I was asked (no voice!) "How much more do you want?" And I was reminded that I'd prayed since B's stroke that she might die first, without having the trauma of loss.
Prayer answered.

In her last days in hospital, Stephanie, Jenny and I agreed to respect B's living will with no medical intervention. I prayed she might go with dignity, without struggle and painless.
Prayer answered.

There were numerous other smaller things.
Prayer answered.

And yet I always seem to want more.

JOURNAL, 8TH JUNE, 2007

Faith – is a gift – of grace.
God gives it. What are the criteria?
Not that anyone deserves it, or earns it, but that in some way one is ready to receive it.
I open my hands, stretch them out for more, but is there some obstacle that blocks a greater gift?
Or do I have it already, unrecognised? If the desire to pray is prayer then maybe the desire to strengthen faith is the faith itself.
I cannot create the conditions under which faith is strengthened, but then who can?

The Holy Spirit already at work within? But it moves by tiny incremental bits of progress. "Lord, I believe, help then my unbelief..."
Maybe unbelief is part of belief, just as doubt is part of faith.

JOURNAL, 13TH JUNE, 2007

I've learned to live with the question, Why does God make loving so painful? and with God's silence. Kathryn, our minister, set me on a train of thought, saying pain is the downside of joy. As though you paid for one by the other. Don't buy that either.

Now, without an answer I arrive at a modus vivandi. If I could lose/avoid the pain and also lose the joy, I wouldn't accept the compromise. But I come to this understanding: that it is the richness of joy, and its intensity which inevitably highlights/intensifies the pain. There is a logic, a yin/yang thing which suggests an inevitability, but in the end, the joy outshines the pain.
And I thank God, and Barbara, for it.

JOURNAL, 26TH JULY, 2007

RUMOURS OF JOY

Over the last two days, I've twice been attacked in unguarded quiet moments with what I can only describe as attacks of a rumour of joy. That joy still exists and that I might yet find it. This sudden, gentle feeling of joy immediately turned into a thank you to God – maybe faith is still alive – even though it may still be battered and weak!
Praise be.

JOURNAL, 4TH AUGUST, 2007
RECEIVED BY GOD

For some time I've been reading a Psalm before getting into bed.
I question many of them where they say e.g. fortress, rock, refuge
etc. because in local, human, immediate terms God obviously wasn't a
rescuer. We then spiritualise it and say "while you may suffer now,
your inner core/spirit is safe."
I suppose we take from the Bible whatever brings us comfort and
encouragement.

LATER

One great encouragement has been the words from a missionary
friend's memorial service in the USA.
Rather than question where B is, where her spirit is, what she does
(none of which we know except the clichés) this says simply...

"She is received by God, with mercy, compassion, grace, forgiveness
and love."

A great comfort, I don't need answers beyond that.

JOURNAL, 6TH AUGUST, 2007

FLOODS

I'm preoccupied with floods – first Gloucester, and now in India
and Bangladesh, and here locally, a regular threat in the village.

A flood wall to be built. Behind the floodwall, water ever seeking,
feeling for the weak spot.

Grief is similar. Probing, searching for the way in (or is it out?). Into
my life, my consciousness. The even keel rocked, the reminders, the
triggers that start the grief again. A little quieter, a little less raw,
but grief alive and strange and looking for another manifestation.

Just picking up a family photo. B with Georgia on her knee, B looking
so proud. That's all it took. The grief – a little gentler, but real –
took over.

The Dove

He was a lovely bird
the collared dove.
The muted grey, the flash of white,
the softness in my hands.
But he flew into the plate glass
of our patio window,
headfirst.
He died quickly, neck broken.
I picked him up,
gently.
The breeze ruffled his feathers
as if a gentle wakening were all he needed,
but the life had gone.
O that I could have loved him back to life.

I am that collared dove.
I fly on wings of faith,
swoop, circle
and in joy
see the world from high
until there is a bump,
an unseen and unexpected obstacle
that brings me crashing down.

Faith flat-on-faced.
And I am grounded.

But still alive
and in the debris of my fall
there's still a flutter of faith to which I cling,
and slowly I will learn to fly again.
Perhaps the dove has gone on ahead
and now he flies in some celestial kingdom,
on stronger wings, flying with God,
flying and rejoicing with God.

I await my eagle's wings.

Eddie Askew, 2007

The death of the dove saddened Dad more deeply because of his love for wildlife. The beauty of this bird and the senseless waste, however small, mattered to him. He rang to ask if we knew a way to avoid a recurrence. We found this poem, The Dove, shortly after he had gone.

Autumn Glow, *watercolour*

Even youths grow tired and weary, and young men stumble and fall; but those who hope in the LORD will renew their strength. They will soar on wings like eagles; they will run and not grow weary, they will walk and not be faint.
Isaiah 40:30–31 (NIV)

Part Three
August 12, 2007

A neighbour rang Steph to say Dad was in hospital with a suspected stroke. The shock and fear flooded in, as we had to accept it had happened again. This was not in our plan. We thought we had Dad for some years yet.

We had plans. Christmas in India. A trip to the Antarctic with Steph. A painting holiday to Venice with me. Daily phone calls. More trips to the Lake District.

Yet again, the lonely journeys up and down the M1. The walking down endless corridors to find him confused in a bed, name tag on his wrist. It was his left side. No movement in his arm. No more beautiful paintings. He was left handed.

We will always be grateful to a close friend of Dad's, Jean, who sat with Jenny, and held her hand in those early days. More rounds of doctors, scans, blood tests, and then physio. The weeks passed and he seemed to make some small progress, though there was great sadness in his eyes. In his words, he felt "this was cruel".

Then, in early September, another call. He had had a series of seizures and was very ill. The staff and doctors were unendingly kind; he was given a side room and we sat with him and waited and watched.

· · ■ ■ ■ ■ · ·

Summer turned to autumn as we sat. Sensing the curling of the leaves outside as they prepared to fall. We felt the loosening of a life well lived, a shifting of tensions in anticipation of what was to come. We wept as we sat, waiting for the wind which would lift him and give him flight, his heart fluttering like a caged bird, poised and ready.

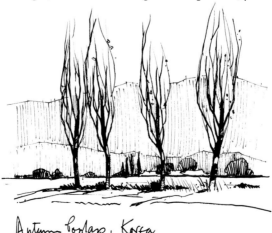

Autumn Poplars, Korea

Jenny wrote this poem as we sat by the bedside, waiting...

For my Father

The air is thick with the
beating of wings.
The Presence close,
the Immortal near.
Perfection meets with frailty,
raising up on eagle's wings,
transforming,
completing that which was
begun in love.
Now full circle,
love meets love,
and all is done,
and all is done,
and all will be well,
and all will be well.

Jenny Hawke

We will always be grateful for the time we had to say goodbye, to say thank you for being the father he was, to simply sit and hold his hand.

· ▪ ▮ ▮ ▪ ·

He died quietly in the early hours of the morning on the 27th September. We were called in and sat with him for a while as we wept. A nurse said she had been with him at the end. She had wanted to. "He was a nice man," she said.

Thank God for her.

He is gone

After Dad's death we again experienced that intense longing, for just one more word, one more hug, one more opportunity to say "I love you."

But deep inside a part of us always knew that 'one more' would never be enough.

· ■ ■ ■ ■ · ·

He's gone.
He's gone.
My magnetic north,
my point of loving reference.

He's gone.
He's gone.
Words echo the sad stillness.
Thoughts bouncing on
brutal walls.
A paradigm shift
of volcanic proportion.
And I am lost.

Jenny Hawke

Dawn, *watercolour*

Help comes in many forms

During the days which followed both Mum and Dad's death, we were overwhelmed by messages coming in from the Christian community across the world, both letters, cards, e-mails and texts.

'On eagle's wings.'
A common theme from Isaiah, 'and they shall rise up on eagle's wings.' People from all over the world sent us this verse, individuals who did not know each other, moved by news of his death. These were words he loved, and he longed for that experience as a reality. There is a palpable tension between the 'here and now' and the longed for 'reality of a heaven', where there are no more tears and no more pain. The image is vivid, the words strengthen if we allow them to, the spirit is touched and hope is stirred.

· ▪ ▪ ▓ ▪ ▪ ·

Many sent personal recollections of times spent with them both; others included Bible verses, or quotes from favourite hymns. Some said very little except to say they were thinking of us. Many people phoned and left short messages for us. Dad's personal assistant for many years phrased our loss beautifully. "It feels as if a huge tree in a forest has fallen, leaving a gap which can never be filled."

Others called Mum and Dad, 'visionaries', and used the words 'Well done, thou good and faithful servant.'

· ▪ ▪ ▓ ▪ ▪ ·

One longstanding friend of theirs sent regular and beautifully worded cards, sometimes every week. We found this such a lovely thing, that someone continued to care as the weeks went by, still finding the time to send them. Thank you, Jenny.

Others sent beautiful flowers filling the rather neglected house with fragrance.

Some came to the house, in spite of the feeling of 'not wanting to intrude', and shared in the tears and hugs, their timing always welcome.

Our church sent flowers and did not mind our weeping. Our Pastor likened grief to the movement of orbiting planets, circular, elliptical, sometimes close, and intensely real, sometimes far away.

We are grateful to so many:

The hospital chaplain who was with us in such a real and daily sense, reminding us that this life is not all there is, that God is 'other' and all-encompassing. We did not need to pretend that we were 'okay' when we were not.

The hospital consultant who encouraged us when we wavered and doubted our decisions about the living will.

Mum and Dad's minister and close friend, Kathryn. Her quiet support and loving acceptance of us was something we came to rely on.

Mum and Dad were blessed with wonderful neighbours, especially Terry and Sandy. They quietly supported Dad through the first weeks of loss, providing meals and company, always making sure he was cared for. Their love and support continued for us after Dad died, and still does.

All were an important part of our grieving. We felt blessed, included, prayed for, and loved.

· ■ ■ ■ ■ ■ ·

If you know someone who is grieving, don't hesitate. Do whatever you are being prompted to do. God seems to take care of the timing. When Dad was in hospital nearing the end of his life, we lost count of the times a friend would text us, often when we felt at breaking point. It helped more than you can imagine. The real meaning of community.

There is a sense in which some people feel the need to avoid the subject for fear of upsetting us, but we found a feeling of relief and strong connection in being able to talk about the person, and still do. It is part of the healing process.

Don't stay silent.

Be brave, hold a hand, send a card, make a cake, leave a message, reach out in whatever way you can...

Another funeral

As before, the planning of his funeral was as much for us as for him. Looking back, it was a positive process as we chose the words Dad loved, the poetry and Psalms. Hymns which in our grief reminded us that God is still God, that wonderful line, 'The Lord gives; the Lord takes away; blessed be the name of the Lord.'

There is both a sanctity and a security in ritual, marking important times in our lives and this was one of the greatest in ours. Again the whole family was involved, encouraged to participate in whichever way they felt able. The funeral was doubly painful, reminding us of the few months before when we waited outside the house for Mum's coffin. Now we did the same for Dad. It was too soon.

During the funeral, Steph read this beautiful Celtic blessing.

His life is finished;
God has received his life,
God has received his life with mercy,
with compassion, with grace,
with forgiveness, with love.
And this is the final word;
addressed to him and addressed to us;
"Nothing shall separate us from the love of God –
In Christ Jesus our Lord."

And once again we read a passage from the final page of *A Pilgrim's Progress*, which includes these wonderful words...

But glorious it was to see how the upper region was filled with horses and chariots, with trumpeters and pipers, with singers and players on stringed instruments, to welcome the pilgrims as they went up, and followed one another in at the beautiful gate of the city.

From A Pilgrim's Progress *by John Bunyan*

The service ended with these wonderful words, read by Kathryn Bracewell, their minister.

Go forth upon thy journey Christian soul! Go from this world.
Go in the name of God, the omnipotent Father who created thee.
Go in the name of Jesus Christ our Lord who bled for thee.
Go in the name of the Holy Spirit who was poured out on thee.
Go in the name of angels and archangels.
In the name of thrones and dominions.
In the name of principalities and powers.
In the name of cherubim and seraphim.
In the name of the Holy Apostles and Martyrs.
In the name of all the saints of God.

And today – let thy place be in peace
through the same Christ our Lord.

Adapted from Elgar's The Dream of Gerontius,
words by John Henry Newman

What a faith we have...

A Celebration of a Life Well-lived

The celebration of his life was at Mum and Dad's church in Nottingham, the room full of friends, many of whom had travelled a long way to be there.

It was a beautiful time; reassuring to hear of the love people had for him, providing a space for us to tell stories about Dad; like the fact that every evening, without fail, he would have a bowl of chocolate ice cream. And the fact that during the war, as a young boy he noticed that when he carefully folded his socks at the end of the day, there would be no air-raid! He realised at the age of 75 he was still doing it! He felt he had proved the point, since there had been no air-raids in Attenborough for many years!

· ▪ ■ ▌ ■ ▪ ·

Again, as a young boy, he joined the Boys' Brigade, conscripted for some strange reason into the band, to play the cornet. Unfortunately, he couldn't play it, but did a good job of pretending to at all the rehearsals, until one day the leader asked him to play a solo. The game was up. He left. We think he saw it as a challenge to keep the pretence up as long as he could!

When he was a frequent flyer, and terrorist attacks were beginning, he would joke about taking his own bomb with him everywhere as the chances of there being two bombs on one plane was incredibly unlikely.

Every Sunday morning, when we were children, we would climb into Mum and Dad's bed, and he would tell us a 'Silver Grey Monkey Story', always beginning the same, and always finishing with us in hysterics. This tradition carried on with our children whenever we visited, the difference being the increasing numbers of children and adults on the bed, listening.

· ▪ ■ ▌ ■ ▪ ·

Many people spoke of their time with him as a leader, speaker and author. Their love and admiration for him made us proud.

It was a fitting tribute to a life well-lived.

Dreams of Life

Dad told me of a dream he once had, shortly after the death of his mother, Gladys, and a few months before the birth of my daughter, Jessamy. Dad was a bit suspicious of dreams, careful not to give them unnecessary significance but I think he was touched and amused by this one.

He dreamt the whole family were sitting up on a high shelf, side by side, legs dangling and all in chronological order. He saw his mother gently drop off one end of the shelf, and at the same time, saw Jessie, the new baby, being placed on at the other end. Everyone shifted slightly to make room for her.

"The endless cycle of life," he told me and smiled.

Dream Cottage, *watercolour*

And the last entry in the journal....

Have felt, am feeling, depressed. It is, I think, the empty space in the house, the spaces which were filled by B. Every time I get up from the bed, I glance sideways to make sure I haven't disturbed her. At least a dozen times a day I turn to share something, some comment, with her. But she is disappointingly, emphatically not there. It's like a door slamming shut in my face just as I am going through it.

Then tonight there was a long TV programme about a man developing Alzheimers and his heroic wife caring for him. Thank God B did not develop that way.

And I have to say from my heart, a genuine thank you to God that He gave us so many wonderful years together, and allowed her to go before anything dreadful might have developed.

Death and loss, and pain of loss, can be a hidden mercy.

Since B died I have, many times, railed against God for the pain of loving and loss; now I trust that my heart-felt THANK YOU can cover the rebellion!

In the months that followed Mum's death, Dad did not have all the answers. His emotions and his understanding of his faith were rocked, sometimes coming in to land fleetingly, and rest in an atmosphere of peace. But as the weeks passed, a more gentle acceptance, and as he put it, "the occasional rumour of joy", became a more welcome part of his life.

This last entry of his heartens us. Although still desperately sad, he had come to a more settled place in his journey through grief, deeply aware of the great blessing of their years together. He was so thankful, and had come to a place of peace.

Living with grief

When Mum died, I made jam. I found a tangible comfort in the process, in the feeling of control over a small and mundane part of my life. My kitchen shelves began to fill.

When Dad died, I began again, collecting fruit wherever I could find it, filling the house with a sweeter smell. My shelves began to sag, and I wrote this.

Jam

When She died, I made jam.
Took comfort in the steady movement.
The chopping, peeling, slicing.
Slow roll of the darkening fruit.
Steam rising in my orange kitchen,
a gentle mix for my tears.

The jam jars stand
nudging shoulders quietly on the shelf,
a promise of sweetness to come.
The tight covers stretch with loving tension
as I hold my breath
waiting to begin again.

Jenny Hawke

Adjustment

This difficult process, this adjustment of our lives has to be. Our society tells us that the loss of parents is a natural process, implying it should be relatively pain-free. Having loved them as we did, we feared the loss but hoped for a gentle transition, but loss is always loss and always painful, as we discovered.

We have no choice but to rejoin our busy lives even before we are ready. The shift internally is massive, the loss enormous, but the journey goes on. We alone can choose how we process and how we remember.

·■■▓■■·

During this time of grieving for our parents, we have learnt, we hope, to be kind to ourselves, giving ourselves time within busy lives to continue grieving, for as long as it feels necessary.

If you are grieving, there will be times when you wake, and all seems normal. The day fills and the sadness of your loss lies light across your shoulders.

And yet there will be days, when no matter how strong the intention, another wave of grief will come, pressing down, taking your breath away. It will take your attention again, and you will pause, and listen, and weep, and wait for it to pass. These are the days where kindness is needed, where expectations must stay soft amongst the bedclothes, as memories beckon, and time stands still by the door. We pause and wait for these days to pass in a bittersweet haze, mystified at the passage of the world without us.

We wait, until hope appears at the door.

Morning Mist, *watercolour*

Dad and Mum's life story is told in his book, *Edge of Daylight*. It finishes with this paragraph, and we see no better way to close this book than in the same way.

The poet Andrew Motion, says the gift of daylight is temporary, its end inevitable. '*Darkness takes the edge of daylight*' he writes...

But it is the darkness that is temporary.

We travel as pilgrims from the little light we have through the darkness into a greater light than we can imagine. That will be the last and greatest adventure of all as we are drawn into the splendour of the full light of God.

From Edge of Daylight, *2000*